BOLD KIDS

Gold Rush

CHILDREN'S EXPLORATION BOOK

No part of this book may be reproduced or used in any way or form or by any means whether electronic or mechanical, this means that you cannot record or photocopy any material ideas or tips that are provided in this book.
Copyright 2022

All images in this book have been reproduced with the knowledge and prior consent of the artists concerned, and no responsibility is accepted by producer, publisher, or printer for any infringement of copyright or otherwise, arising from the contents of this publication.

The first step in understanding the Gold Rush is to understand why it happened. While most people who made the journey were able to make some money, others spent their savings and mortgaged property.

Men were willing to risk the dangers of mining, but few of them became rich. Women were more entrepreneurial and set up hotels and dance halls, which many miners needed for the long trip. This makes the Gold-Rush a fascinating story for kids to learn about.

It was also important to understand that merchants made more money from the gold than the miners did. This is because the California Gold Rush lasted from 1848 to 1855. Some of the great industrialists of America made their start in this time.

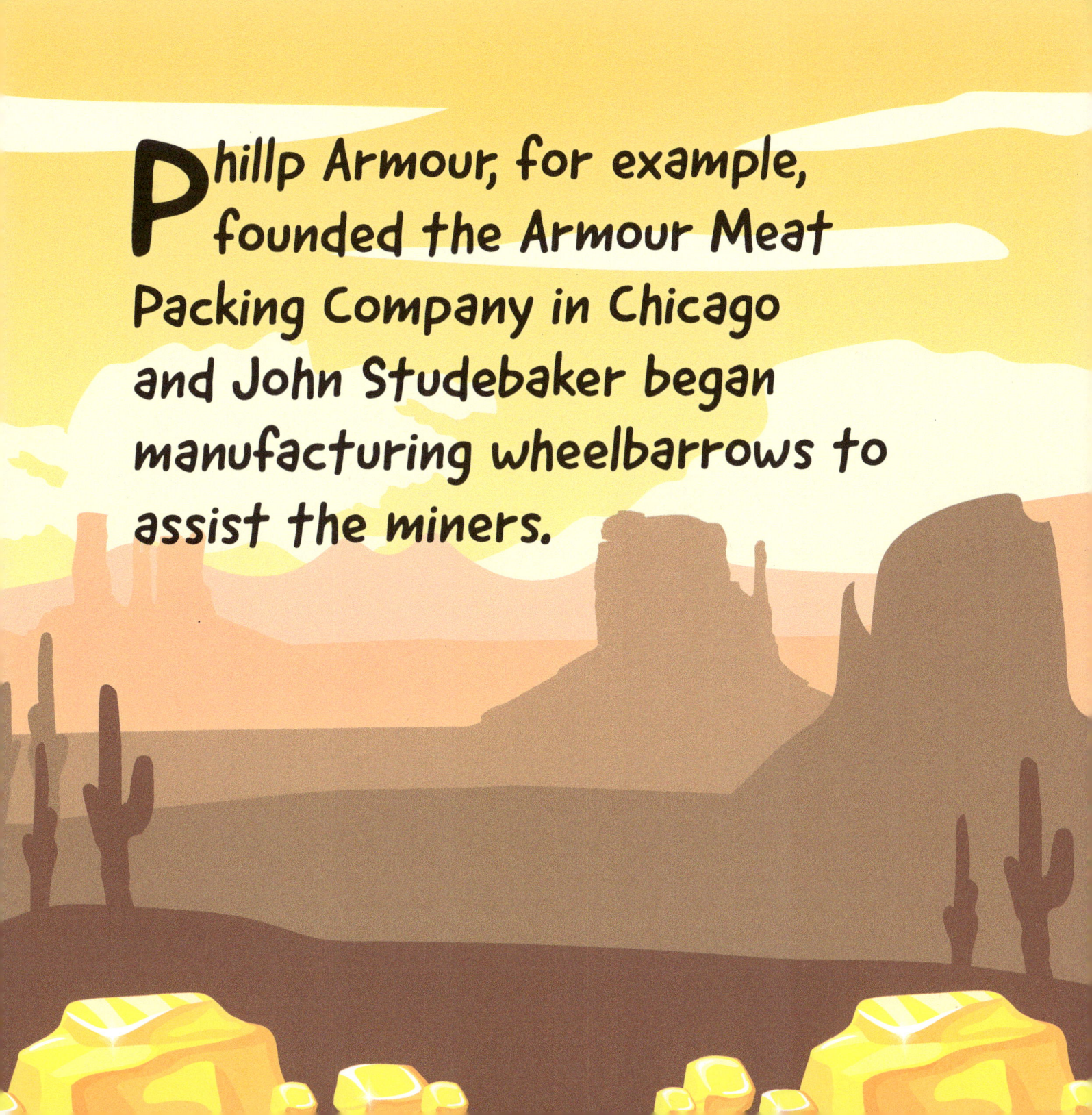

Phillp Armour, for example, founded the Armour Meat Packing Company in Chicago and John Studebaker began manufacturing wheelbarrows to assist the miners.

A third group of people who made their fortunes during the Gold Rush were the merchants. Many of the great industrialists of today got their start in the gold rush. Some of them built large companies by selling their own goods.

Phillp Armour, for example, grew his meatpacking empire in Chicago while John Studebaker produced wheelbarrows for gold miners. This was a big event in the American history of commerce and the development of America.

Besides the miners, the merchants were also making fortunes. The gold rush provided a great opportunity for some of America's greatest industrialists. Phillp Armour, for example, founded the Armour Meatpacking Company and built a meatpacking empire in Chicago.

Likewise, John Studebaker made wheelbarrows for the miners. So, while the miners may have been the ones responsible for finding the gold, the merchants made more money than the miners did.

Thousands of people arrived in California during the Gold Rush. The town had to be built from scratch. Businessmen needed to feed, clothe, and supply the miners. A Bavarian tailor, Levi Strauss, came to California in 1850 to make tents and wagon covers.

He designed pants that were sturdy and comfortable for the miners. The new material was eventually transformed into blue jeans. It's important for young children to learn about the Gold-Rush.

While the miners made the majority of the profits, merchants also made the most profit from the Gold Rush. Some of the most influential industrialists in America got their start during the GoldRush.

Hemingway.com offers eleven worksheets on the Gold-Rush. These are sure to be the most valuable and fun educational materials for your students! They will love this learning resource and the history behind it!

The California Gold-Rush is a fascinating history lesson for kids. The Californian gold rush saw more than $750,000 worth of gold. In 1852, the first time gold was discovered in the U.S., but the news took years to get to the eastern coast.

The early immigrants came from all over the world. The first people who settled in California were immigrants from China. When the supply of the precious metal dried up, anti-immigrant tensions were high and the government had to intervene.

The California Gold Rush had a great impact on the local population and the environment. Chemicals used during the mining process killed fish and destroyed habitats in the area. The state had to develop its own roads and towns.

The Gold Run had a great impact on the economy of California and the world. The Gold Rush also made California the most prosperous state in the country. The Californian state was born from this gold rush.

The Gold Rush was a period of rapid change in the history of the West. It brought prosperity to the people of California. Thousands of *immigrants* poured into the state.

As a result, California's first millionaires were among the people who arrived in California during this time. It also led to the development of railroads and steamships. The boom in the gold rush made California a major center for commerce.

Ingram Content Group UK Ltd.
Milton Keynes UK
UKHW050453050723
424548UK00008B/69